Dedicated
to *All*

Mary Caiello

PAGE PUBLISHING, INC.
New York, NY

First originally published by Page Publishing, Inc. 2017

ISBN 978-1-64027-051-0 (Paperback)
ISBN 978-1-64027-052-7 (Digital)

Printed in the United States of America

Dedicated to All

May God Bless You

Depth

Developing endless pathways through hope
Saying that you hope, you can, is well on your way,
to being able to do all that you already are endowed with,
but yet need to have a path to perform on.

"For every path there lies a performance under the direction of truth!"

Pebbles beneath your feet
sometimes seeming like rocks
Oh, how nice when you
get to the sand
Smooth and tingly between
your toes
ENJOY for the feeling
can be yours.

"Allowing yourself to have faith that all can and shall have beauty, is your greatest gift to yourself."

ENJOY
Forever

"Musget"

To be of now with, changes so many,
My mind, wonders, to great degree,
To be of now, with changes so many,
My body scrambles, to only flee.

Get it together – no slowdown
Do you get it together or make few sounds?

Speak up! I can't hear you,
No – wait, and be quiet.
I can't understand why you
Must stay so silent!

Do as you're told or, do you
do as you feel?
You must get it together, to find
what is REAL,
Open your heart, be prepared
for alarm,
When the disguise disappears
You
       will
          be
          faced
             with
                 no
                    harm.

"The answers unfamiliar areas, are waiting with open arms of peacefulness."

Standstill

'Twas morning when I first heard the cars, the people, the whistle of the wind, and brightly through the drapes, I could see the rays of brightness, the light of the sun shining. A yawn and stretch, they together were of one, then a roll here, a toss there, to only bring myself to a stand. Reaching for shorts, trying to find a top to match still left unknowing where I had laid my sandals. It's spring, joyous spring, time of life, but yet what was it that keeps me from smiling? A day had passed, today was here, yet something, was wrong. Oh well, not important enough to remember, but yet enough to trouble me. Something, but yet nothing. Oh, well tomorrow, yes, always tomorrow. Too nice of a day to think too nice of a day to spend wondering. So yes, my shoes, wherever! Under the bed, one but not two. Yes, behind that box there it is. Good old shoes! To laugh, to laugh loud, to feel and to touch, to see what is there, to know that all can be done. Exit, you must leave, go out so you may find, walk so you may step on the grass, the stones, and in the water. Move, you can't stand still, move so you can experience, all that you have to be a part of! Stop—no, no such word, never any ending. I can't even leave my room! Darkness, where did that bright spark of light go? It's fading!

The refreshingness is gone yet a calmness, but yet fearful feeling. Better take off my shoes and put them back, so I may know, that I can try tomorrow. Again, tomorrow is here. I try, but it is raining. I couldn't go with the sun; how do I expect to leave with the rain? YESTERDAY, TODAY, TOMORROW, no matter what, they are all here now, and yet, nothing seems to be moving anywhere!

"Serine Trepidation as Newness Develops Souls Trenchant Incommutable Limpid Love."

Self

Just as a bird has its song to sing
So does a bell with its outgoing ring,
Forever and ever, shall we always hear,
The words of togetherness, without any fear.

When nighttime comes, and there is no one around
Allow yourself to not think, there is no sound to be found
Just speak to yourself, without any doubt,
Be ready to be answered, when you hear a shout,

That all is well, and you shall see
That deep inside us all we have the key,
Just take the time, to believe in you
For yourself can be your very own school.

"You are never alone. If you believe, you have yourself."

Prolonged
    Attentiveness
        Through
            Intense
                Encompassment
                Nearing
                    Changeable
                        Enticement

To have the will, to be able to wait
No matter the happening, no matter how late,
Allowing yourself time, to actually see,
that time is on your side, for you to be,
Forever knowing there is time to do
Everything that you would really like to.
No need for rushing, for each moment is there,
To help yourself out, and show others you care.

"Patience – instilled throughout time, as an endless calmness."

He

  who

    walks

      in

        a

          path

            of

              darkness

              Shall

            go

          on

         walking

       without

    the

      bright rays of the

      SUNLIGHT

"May it be easier to travel with the light on, rather than it being turned off."

How great it feels, at the end
of the day,
To be able to look back, and
truly say,
There are so many people, whom
you know are friends
For they will always be with
you, right to the end,
They won't back down for they
are ready to take their stand,
In any way offering you, a helping
hand.

"Knowing how good it feels, when you can feel just how good you feel about yourself, knowing how good it feels, when you can have someone else feel good about themselves, and knowing just how good it feels, when someone else helps you to feel that they care is truly feeling, a feeling of worth."

When unaware, of your inner feelings

You can find yourself

With no direction

The harder you look the more distant you get

Give it time and be patient, you should

never regret.

Those days that you waited, so patiently,

From the time of question, to eternity.

"Allowing yourself time, to make sure, that the key which you hold,
opens the door of your choice!"

Seemingly as yet
    question still ponders my mind
Go out
    and search
       for your answers
       Although
the day will come
when all questions will
    be senseless
Because all answers shall be!

    "Question? Answer. Each has its own!"

Control

To know control is to acknowledge to yourself as being able to maintain responsibility, and to know that, you being of strength will help you to see that responsibility can be a passive art from within only to blossom through: listening clearly, feeling sensitively, seeing deeply, touching directly, thinking objectively, allowing expression having taste and aroma become as one, and most of all allowing all that is, to *be*, without judgment.

"Question not

   what you feel

      you can do

         for yourself

            just

         allow yourself room to do for

            you."

Teacher

A person who guides, with no intention to lead
While helping others to grow, within
their own speed.
Offering advice when needed in
a very positive way.
Allowing time for another, to
be able to say.
Just whatever it is, that they
may be feeling.
Then helping them, to express it
move freely.
When it is understood as to
what they want to do
What becomes the very next step,
is up to you!

"Taking out time to help another to learn, and waiting for them to
understand, *is* truly CARING!"

Knowing
    Myself
       as me
           being true

    and

Knowing
    that I
      and me
         is of one

How great I feel
    knowing that
      me *is*!

"Learn to know yourself and you shall truly learn, to love yourself."

Setup

Man's games go around
    with what seems to
        be a never-ending stop,
Not saying for harm
    but yet the games
        play back and forth.
Why can't man tell,
you he cares without
        playing his games?

"To say just what you feel, to be the truth, *is* indeed, your shortest
path to settle your conscience."

Moon

"Magical omen originally nocturnalized."

May forever the moon, enhance a
mystery of beyond
For it shall gaze, through the night,
with its light aglow,
As you stand and watch its
brightness shine
Let its essence maintain a paradise
for those of wizardry.

"May the moon reflect upon us, as our mirror to mysticism."

S	**u**	**m**	**m**	**e**	**r**
p	n	e	e	t	a
e	c	m	a	e	m
c	o	o	s	r	i
i	n	i	u	n	f
f	d	r	r	a	i
i	i	s	e	l	c
c	t				a
	i				t
	o				i
	n				o
	a				n
	l				s

"Treasure thy steps, which are of direct, demonstrative pleasure.
Enjoy FUN!"

Multiple Divinity

Measuring ultimate living things, intensely placed, lending eternal, divine, intriguing, vending, internalized newness, inwardly through yearning.

"Depth has been given to all, so that each one's unique soul may be developed to its ultimate height."

Whisper

As silent as a grain of sand, becoming more of what already is, while travelling through time, as it being that of a spaceless age, leaving particles as it grows, toward a becoming of more!

"Move with sound, move with a whisper, just as long as you move!"

Peace

"Pacification entailing absolute capitulation effectively"
Peace, a feeling which tells you that *all* is all right,
Peace a feeling which takes away any fright,
Peace a feeling which helps you to feel okay,
Peace a feeling which makes all right in *all* ways.

"To feel peace, is to ultimately ease yourself truly."

Wisdom

Wisdom is acknowledgment, background, capability, decisiveness, ensurement, feeling, general, harmony, ideal, judgment, knowledge, language, measurement, neutral, openness, precise, equality, remembering, simplicity, truth, understanding, virtual, worth, x-ray, yielding, zenith.

"Come to know your wisdom and you shall truly come to learn about yourself."

Wisdom – when intelligence surpasses direct openness momentarily.

Faded

Color, one of life's imbalances
see me, I'm just like you
Open your heart, save me
some chances
I long to want to need, and
to have just like anyone to know
Give me an opening, so that,
someday can show
Life can be easier with more
happiness for us,
Just give me that break for you
and me to adjust.

"Equality *is* life's equation for *all*!"

Not many word for a
time like this
when hurt is felt so strong

Yet answers to questions
you need right now
But the time to know seems
to take so long

"For all who ask within themselves, shall always find their truest answer, when they truly become ready.

Listening carefully to yourself and others, is your key to the door
KNOWING."

Prayer

pacific

reserve

    acknowledging

        your

            estimated

            religion

"prayer is there for all, at all times, and at any place, that anyone wishes to pray."

with *ETERNITY*

of your existence

And sharing the reminder

Throughout the air

Only letting yourself burst

In all shapes colors and sizes

the sky

up toward

So – freely you float

Bubble

"Releasing of yourself, to your beauty which you hold in, virtually
shall only bring peace."

Goodbye

So hard to say such a small word, and lesser a task to so easily do for the time you were here all the great times we did share, your love which you offered to me, as well as my love which I offered to you.

Please take care of yourself, as I shall too, for our love to each other, was and is true.

"Parting doesn't mean ending and never shall it be!"

To know peace is to know that you are:
___, blessed, caressed, delighted, embraced, faithful, gently, holy, independent, jubilant, knowing, ___, matured, nourished, opened, ___ quiet, radiant, safe, ___, united, valid, worthy, ___, you, zestful.

"May
      Peace
            Forever
                  Be
                        With
                            You."

Marriage Oath

There is no need to mention as to what you look like to me, for all I shall see is your beauty.

Many words shall at length be spoken, but none other than love shall I speak.

My truest treasures will be of the moments that I touch you, for they shall contain my truest feelings from within.

All shall hear of my deepest thoughts of you, by listening to your presence as ours.

I shall comfort my soul with your warmth, so that a blanket of cover shall never be needed.

My stand will be of that which will always be by your side, only to know that we are together as one.

For all these things, do take thee, as my love forever!

"Allow yourself to cherish love, and love shall cherish you forever!"

Trust

Truth rebuilds ultimate
salvation totally

To trust is to totally believe that you or another shall only lead you on to the path of truth.

"So may it be that all shall learn to trust themselves or another or both."

Children, oh my children, come forth to me today, let yourself know, let yourself grow, to see that today is our day, For ___ the world passeth over, to another time zone, let us believe that our Almighty is known.

"As you passeth over, you shall know truly that *I am alive!*"

Thank You

Thank you for being a person who cares,
Thank you for being someone who is not afraid to share,
Thank you for allowing someone's ___ existence to be,
Thank you for your kindness, which sets one heart aglow,
Thank you for your honesty when the truth is told,
Thank you for your love, which we endlessly hold,
Thank you for being a true friend we adore,
Thank you for not holding back but giving much more,
Thank you for the times that we spend with each other
Thank you for your beauty which enquisitely loves
Thank you for being *YOU*.

"To be thy self, *can* and *shall* bring only the very best to surface."

Start
    As
        Your
            Beginning
        As
    An
End
        Never
Ending
    And
        All
            That
                Is
            In
        Between
    is

"A step forward, a step backward, a step downward, a step upward, no matter in what direction you may step, you are still stepping."

A - Z
For Happiness

Happiness is acceptance
        belief
caring
developing
enjoyment
freedom
giving
homeland
insight
joy
kindness
love
meaning
newness
opportunity
peace
quest
rendering
smiling
trust
universality
veracity
wisdom
x-mas
yearning
zest

"All shall forever experience some form of happiness at all times."

No matter the distance, no matter the length of time, shall we remember always, our memories of you and me,

Some really happy, oh how we laughed and shared, all of our moments of which we truly cared.

Yes, there are memories of times we both must say that if there were another chance, maybe, we would do things another way.

But yet, even if we could maybe, we would never really want to redo, what was truly needed as best friends, for me and for you.

Best friends

"You and me, me and you, forever!"

Time

T i m e
i   Time
m   T i m e
e   i

      m

      e

     TIME
Through intense moments evolving

    "My
    time
     is
   your time
    for
     us
   to share
    our
    time
with each other"

Time Time
  Time
Time i Time
i m i
m e m
e   e

God in his own fashion, who has made life be forever, has given unto all souls the knowing that their existence shall never cease and for all to forever behold the truth that for whatever they may question unto themselves there forever lies within their truest answers. Rise all so that you may never ponder in one place too long for your path is such that no pebbles should be left unturned and that as the winds help to carry you along unto your final destination that being your becoming of your beginning, you and God shall always have a song together for life whether it be on earth, or throughout the heavens.

"As you await for me, I as well await for you. Your becoming is my becoming!"

S **U** **N** **S** **H** **I** **N** **E**
a n i p a n e v
c i r i r r e e
r v v r m v n r
e e a i o a n l
d r n t n t e a
s a d i a s s
a s e o d t
l d u i
l s n
l g
y

"Shall
The
Bright
Rays
Of
The
sunshine
overcome
darkness
when
light
is
needed"

Cloud

Oh delicate cloud, as you go
passing by
Way so far up, in our wondrous
Sky,
Knowing where you are destined,
for you are your guide,
By sweeping up particles, so you
So upholdingly stride,
    Your path being so such, in so
Many different ways,
    To help you to caress the earth,
Each and every day

Celestial Lambent oblation ultimately descended!

"To conquer the universe, you must step upon your path to
enchantment."

Voyage

Picture yourself sailing
    across the open sea
Let yourself feel
    that gentle breeze
Knowing that your captain
    will show you your way
With not a care in the world
    on such a sunshine day
Allow gently sail over
    the sea today!

"To *BE* on to *BECOME* awaits for when you are ready!"

(Scientist)

S
c
i
e
n
t
i
s
t

Someone who likes to question
About all that there is
It doesn't matter about shape
or color
Oh whether or not
Something is sharp or dull

Only   just   he is
   he   what   to
     knows   area   cover

And that his job is not done

Until

his answer is found!

"To grow *is* to ___ know that growing to knowing *is* beautiful."

Friend

To be able to be someone whom, you could really
say you like,
To be able to think of them, and feel
happy within,
To have someone understand you, especially
in friendship that will never part,
To have distance between you, without
losing your closeness,
To take pride in saying, that *we* are true friends.

"To *CARE is* to *SHARE*, and to *SHARE is* to *CARE*. May ALL CARE to SHARE, ALL which they truly CARE about, with one another."

Chance

So much more can be offered
when all take part,
Let somebody see just what
Is in your heart,
Then you can be as free
as a bird,
Just when you are ready,
   shout out the word,
Tell someone else just how
you feel and don't play games,
When you are through, you will
have found a
friend!

"Involvement takes time, and so that is one reason why, ALL have been given their own time."

Spring

Spreading
    Preciosity
        Rendering
            Impassioned
                Newness
                    Glorified

"May all step out of depth, for even a very short time, just so they may breathe, a bit of SPRING air!"

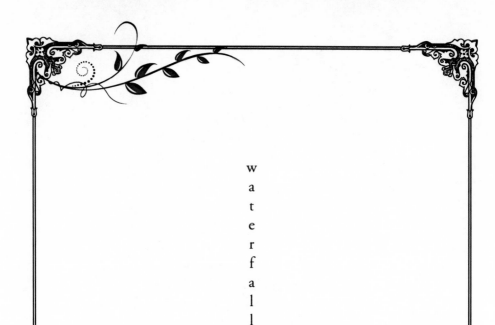

w
a
t
e
r
f
a
l
l

May the coolness of its waters suspend downward, into an ever-lasting moment of togetherness, with eternity's flow.

"Like the waterfall, allowing its flow to become a part of eternity so shall you learn to allow yourself to flow with life!"

Trees
Treasure Remembering Eternity
Instills Serenity

Trees somber in the ground, so
durably we stand
Out in the openness of air, far
and beyond all in compare,
To reach to our heights or to
lower ourselves so far below
Let us tell you of our strength,
by way of means and show,
So much in our makeup, we
take pride in our growth,
No matter how fast, no
matter how slow
For nothing else matters, except
our soul backbone to be
The results we look forward to
that being the most beautiful tree

"The strength of that which is within a single seed, supports an
arranged dimension of growth."

Fear

To fear is to allow yourself to believe that you can be hurt. Therefore, instead learn to allow yourself to believe that fear cannot hurt you. Fear, in turn, will then be able to help you, to set yourself free!

FEAR   or   FREE
Forever Escaping Affirmative   Flexibility Releases
Reasoning   ___ Evermore

"Once you pass through the state of fear, you shall forever realize, that all is of goodness and no harm is awaiting you."

Parting

You have shared of yourself in so many
special ways
That it is our turn now, to share with
you today,
Our love which has grown along with
the faith we know,
That the very best is wished for wherever
you go
So gentle has your smile been which
you have worn upon your face,
An expression of caring, no one will
ever be able to erase.
You will forever be our someone so
special to us,
And we know we will see you again
this we trust
Forever everlasting you will be kept
close to our hearts,
No matter the distance, while we
are apart,
If you ever feel low, and need a
rise to be
Remember how much we love you and
our thoughts for you we carry!

"Distance short or long can still hold true, memories spent by
me or you!"

A is for always we shall be

B is for the best which we hold each day,

C is for caring, about one another

D is for developing, what God has given

E is for everyone to be a part of eternity

F is for Father, to whom we can pray

G is for the goodness, which has been instilled

H is for home where we shall all return

I is for me, to know I exist

J is for the Jesus, whom is inside us all

K is for kindness, how nice it feels

L is for love, the true feeling of closeness

M is for the most, to be given each day

N is for all, to never not know

O is for only, be as you

P is for precious, which we all are

Q is for quest, which leads us to God

R is for real, which is all in existence,

S is for song, so words can travel

T is for time, which we all have been given,

U is for us, to become as one

V is for very special are we,

W is for wisdom which is inside us all

X is for the cross, which ___ around,

Y is for you, to enjoy yourself

Z is for zealous, to just be!

A, B, C, can be as easy as

1, 2, 3 only asking, can be your *answer*.

Belief

A knowing from deep within which tells you that,
your thought is true, and no one else, can say it is theirs
for its meaning, is meant, for only you.
It can be your guide when in doubt,
to only express it lets it out,
and when you have done this, you can truly say,
that what was deep inside, is your very own way!

"All shall know, within their own rightness, that which is, *is* true."

?

Who am I?

What do I want?

Where am I going?

What am I looking for?

Will I be happy? How can I tell?

Questions and more questions,

Will they ever be answered?

Have I been there?

Am I there now?

Will I be there tomorrow?

Will I stay there for long?

What is there? What is for long?

More questions to ever will

they be answered?

How does a person make it,

    In

        A

           World

          So

               Constantly

                   changing?

"All have chosen, their ways along their own paths learn to accept the positive, of which *change* offers."

GLOXINIA
Gaiety Lingers Over Xaxis
Imperishable Nondenominational
In Aphorism

"To live freely, with your attachment belonging, to the life, you have chosen to live. *So Be It.*"

Doll - House

Inside my little dollhouse,
I sit with all of my friends,
There's a Lilly, who is my duck,
Then Charley, who is my moose,
We can't forget, Betty and Jean
They are one as we all know
And if it weren't for Henry, my
most cuddly bear,
My dollhouse, wouldn't be complete.

"To truly feel happy, about where you are at, is truly, an important gift to yourself."

Game for Now

We were together so long how can this be
I learned to love you and you learned to love me
We gave so much to each other it doesn't seem fair
That now you are gone, and I'm not sure where,
We said goodbye to each other, in our own way
But my love for you, has continued to say
"It is so hard for me to let you go
But someday, together we'll be this I know."

"Moving on doesn't have to mean, going away forever!"

You

I am so glad you are you,
in every way
What a nice feeling,
you give me each day,
When you are with me,
or when we're apart,
No matter wherever
you are deep in my heart,
You helping me as well
as I helping you,
Showing each other that,
our love is so true,
How happy am I to
know that we are together,
To share all that we have,
with one another
So special are you, I
want you to know,
That every day my love
for you continues to grow.

"So nice to know that there are others that are nice to know."

Wishing Well

Oh, delightful little wishing well, how
you hold my dreams today,
For all I want, or think I need, to
you in God's name I truly pray,
That each and every moment my
hopes and dreams come true,
With all my little wishes, I openly
say to you,
Oh, delightful little wishing well,
I wish you well today,
May all of your dreams and wishes
come to you along your way."

"Wish – wanting
feeling
secret
happening."

You
walking
your
path
by
yourself
The pebbles beneath your feet,
sometimes seeming like rocks,
Oh, how nice
 when you get to the sand,
Smooth and tingly between your toes,
So nice to rest, but yet what is it
that you think you see over yonder,
Oh, it's hard to leave let alone
say goodbye not knowing
where you're off to,
But since you're not the type to sit
still for long,
Venture
out
knowing
you
will
someday
RETURN

"Enjoy your circle, for it is meant for you to encompass."

"Friends"

Two people who care about one another
Two people to share in things done together
Two people with heart that are willing to give
Two people to help the times how hard they may be
We'll always remember the good you and me!

"May no one ever be without a friend."

Forever
    when
        the
            winds

Cross over beyond the falls
Shall the waters of eternity flow.

"May ALL, within their own rightness of time, come to know that the winds of eternity carry, an immeasurable distance of serenity."

Oh, hazy day, you've come
my way,
As I look at you, I wonder
why,
But yet I know, that in
my heart,
You best of all give me my
start!

"Yesterday
Today
      Tomorrow
are all days with
  new beginnings,
     let your day
         entertain you."

Brother

A long time ago, you entered my heart,
Little to know we began our start
Two people to share, in time and place,
A smile on, each other's face.

I learned to love you, and you learned
to love me,
But yet we couldn't let each other see,
Our feelings which we kept inside,
Our feelings that, we felt to hide,

Yours and my susceptibility to conditioning,
Was the cause of this, all the times we
have missed,
We can't go back and do over again,
But yet we can start, from here on in,

Let's pick up our pieces, for we have
only begun,
There is no more need, for us to run,
We can take our time, and hopefully we
shall see,
That our love for each other, can now be
set free,

"To LOVE *is* to, share your ALLNESS, with ALL, al-ways!"

"Winter"

WAITING
INTENSE
NEWNESS
THROUGH
ETERNAL
   E
   V
         E
   L
   A
   T
   I
   O
   N

"Let thy blanket be of warmth and purity."

Dreamer

Thinking about, the day to come,
    when all of your wishes may
        come true,
Setting aside, the one initial fact,
    that the present holds, much in
        store for you
___ the thought of you being as of now,
    and not of the time when you
        feel somehow,
___ tomorrow will be of
    your dreams at your door, but
    that the time is now, for you
        to explore,
___ for all that which is within, let it
    flow out, so you may begin,
    your journey toward reaching,
        for the stars,
that part of life
    which you have adored,
        was so!

"Life *is* the success of *ALL*."

Wanderer

Being at a pace, where your footsteps travel over hills through the water and letting the wind, whirl around sweeping you softly, to unknown surroundings lending you to not question for you have no request, for any answers.

So gently, you allowing yourself to so freely be saying to all that you know there is a lot to experience but yet you would rather leave it untouched for the present and still keeping space and time open for when your wandering becomes still then maybe you will be ready, to begin a new interest.

"Only when your ready, shall your next step become a part, of your eternal destination."

Today, for just this day has been set aside for you to say to the world, how nice it feels to know that I have been given a chance, for me to become more.

"Take hold of your today and your tomorrow, shall follow with ease."

Golden Silence

So much may all learn, as he
lives each and every day
While taking the time to help
    another out in some special way,
May it forever be said, that
    life is each and all's dream.
And forever shall learning to know,
    unconditionally seems,
That when the going gets tough, and
    no cold comfort can be found,
Let it be forever offered through truth,
    where there is no need for sound.

"Silence – Serenity inhibits
    legendary entity,
    necessitating curative
    enrichment."

Like the strings in a ball, all threaded so tightly, crisscrossed over and over.

Take one end, and start to unravel it, but don't let it drop to the ground, for you shall see, when

you

look

down

on

"Even an entasis, may make you look twice!"

Flight

Oh, yellow butterfly, so softly I felt your wings, as you gently f l u t t e r e d by. So nice of you, to pass along my path, so nice of you, to share of yourself on such a sun-shiny day.

"Take time to notice the smaller things in life, for they when added up shall bring you your most pleasurable moments."

Insight

     Ideal

Neutral

Searching

Imprints

Genuine

Harmony

throughout

A feeling which says that what you believe is true, can be meant for another or for just you. By listening to yourself even when you may be in doubt, gives your feeling a release, to help it come out. It shall guide your way, when you seem to be unsure; it shall lend you to the truth, as your universal cure.

"Believe in insight for insight shall help you to truly believe."

Birth

My birth of God, thank you for
letting it be
If it weren't for you, I know, I could
never have been me,
So beautiful are you, and all which
you have created,
Never let it be known, that I never
stated
"I know that you are there, and I
know that I am,"
Forever shall I be, a part of all
which is within.

"Your birth being of my birth and my birth being of your birth,
Happy Birthday To Us."

R E S P E C T such an important aspect of oneself, but yet it becomes so easily to not see that others have the same all have been granted by God, this quality to experience and to self as being. Go forth and let respect for yourself be understood. Also along your path, when there is another that you see, who has found this quality of respect within and has chosen to let it be known, see him as one, who has earned his right to <u>self-dignity</u>.

"Respect thyself and others, and others shall respect themselves and you!"

F
A
L
L

Forever Affirmative Love Lives

"Nothing is ever lost for all is within its own place."

Evolve

Variation

Overwhelming

Letting

"May ALL *LOVE* ALL all ways forever

May ALL *LOVE* ALL all ways

May ALL *LOVE* ALL

May ALL *LOVE* !"

S
U
R
V
I
V
A
L
Struggling
undauntedly
recalling
vigorously
impressive
validating
activating
longing!

"Survival is living past a moment that you felt you could never survive."

Strength

Knowing that you are, willing to be,
Stating the fact that you are, ready to see,
That there, is a lot, of work to be done,
Saying to yourself there is no need to run
Helping those, who hold despair,
Letting all know, how much you care,
Standing upright no matter how long
Showing the strength you've been given as
Strong!

"*Believing* you can *is* half the battle. Doing what you believe you can *do is* the end of the battle."

LOVE
Here there or wherever
It doesn't matter, as long as it's
together,
under around or on top
If you keep it together, it won't ever

s

t

o

p

You're in charge, of where you want to go,
Just say the word, and let it
grow
you and I, and all that are,
can stop it now, or
forever
go
f a r

"BOUNDARIES are set by LIMITATIONS."

I speak to you, oh can't you hear me,
I look at you, oh don't you see me,
I reach for you, please let me touch you,
For all I want, is for you, to be my friend.

You speak to me, oh yes I hear you,
You look at me, oh yeah I see you,
You reach for me, yeah I do feel you,
For all I want, is for you, to be my friend.

As a friend, I really need you as my friend
As a friend, I really want you as my friend,
As a friend, I'd really like to know you as a friend,

Won't
you
please
give
us
a
chance?

"When someone seems, as if they do not understand, maybe it is you, who can't seem to find a way, to help them show, that they do!"

Speed

Through God our Father, we shall all take heed, for it is he who has established, for us our speed.

What as being fast,

such *that* as being

slow only through God, can anyone know

He has set our pace, and as you will see – there is no race – for all shall return back home

t
o
g
e
t
h
e
r

"All shall return home in their own rightness, and I shall be waiting to welcome you."

Horizon –
Heavens
obliquity
      ridging
      into
           zonal,
          omniscient
               newness!

"From our center we came, and to our center shall return.
SO BE IT."

1 is for me, to keep as I

2 is for another, to walk by my side,

3 is for knowing I have a choice,

4 is for keeping even as nice,

5 is for allowing me, to grow by myself

6 is for giving me, a partner again

7 and beyond tells the story as true.

That above and beyond all, is for me, and for you.

'So nice to walk, your path alone,

So nice to walk, your path with a friend,

So nice to have a path to walk,

So nice to be able to walk,

Enjoy yourself, enjoy another,

Just learn to

ENJOY!"

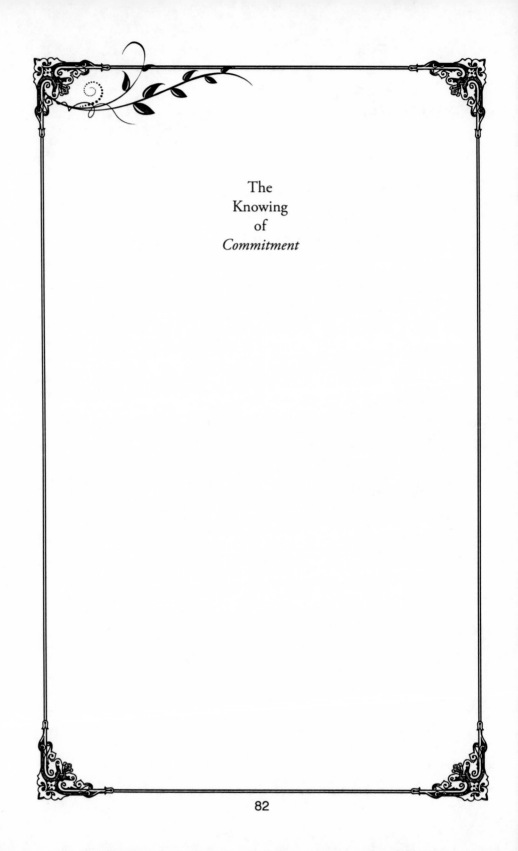

The
Knowing
of
Commitment

About the Author

Hi! My name is Mary A. Caiello. Throughout my life God has placed me in many different experiences. I am fortunate to say that with his love I have made it through them. When I question, I know he is true in giving. When I was very young, I began writing his words only to end up leading with the answers yes, oh yes, "I Am." A brief saying, I want to know, for God shall show.

CPSIA information can be obtained
at www.ICGtesting.com
Printed in the USA
LVOW12s2112100717

540827LV00001B/193/P